Law of

Dedication.

Law of Dedication.

Series "Laws of the Universe "
By: Sherry Lee
Version 1.1 ~December 2023
Published by Sherry Lee at KDP

All information in this book has been carefully researched and checked for factual accuracy. However, the author and publisher make no warranty, express or implied, that the information contained herein is appropriate for every individual, situation, or purpose and assume no responsibility for errors or omissions.

The reader assumes the risk and full responsibility for all actions. The author will not be held responsible for any loss or damage, whether consequential, incidental, special, or otherwise, that may result from the information presented in this book.

All images are free for use or purchased from stock photo sites or royalty-free for commercial use. I have relied on my own observations as well as many different sources for this book, and I have done my best to check facts and give credit where it is due. In the event that any material is used without proper permission, please contact me so that the oversight can be corrected.

TABLE OF CONTENTS.

INTRODUCTION.

So many people today attempt to improve their lives and those around them by becoming the person they were always intended to be.

Utilizing the law of dedication, you can determine if you are prepared to change your life and, more importantly, if you are willing to take action. Even though some will attempt to make this appear easy because it is in their financial interest to do so, this is not entirely accurate.

Dedication requires a genuine desire for change; therefore, the greater your desire and passion for personal development, the greater your likelihood of success. However, the rewards are immense if you are willing to work consistently. Until you embark on this lifelong journey -- for that is what it is -- you will be unaware of what is possible.

You will begin to recognize your potential almost immediately, and as you develop it, it will gradually become an integral part of you. Soon, a new, never-before-seen you will emerge, truly energizing and inspiring you, propelling you forward with remarkable momentum.

But this is not a quick cure; it requires dedication and determination. However, the changes you experience can be so profound that they become irresistible, even though self-growth and development are inherently difficult. Self-empowerment is the most rewarding and interesting work you will ever undertake.

If you're interested in getting the things you've always desired out of life and becoming the person you want to be and ought to be, read on. Imagine for a moment what it would feel like to be able to eliminate all your limiting beliefs and live a truly beautiful and exciting existence. If this appears unfeasible, it is not.

This is how you were born, liberated, and without the limitations and negative beliefs about yourself that others have convinced you are the truth. You have spent your entire existence believing them to be true. You have been programmed with these lies and misinformation about yourself, and your subconscious accepts what is told without question.

You were created with exceptional abilities to become the person you were destined to be. Find out how you can regain access to your innate capabilities, which are your birthright, but you have been denied access through no fault of your own utilizing the law of dedication.

Let's get started.

CHAPTER 1: HOW DID YOU GET HERE? ARE YOU DEDICATED?

This is not a philosophical question posed by a university professor. A young businessman who figured out the answer to this question at a very young age and pursued his ambitions regardless of his misfortunes posed this question. This entrepreneur devoted his life to a goal that everyone around him deemed "impossible."

I am aware of why I am on this planet, and this understanding has helped me endure some of the darkest, cruelest periods of my life when it seemed there was no hope and nothing left to live for.

I understood that it was all part of a plan and that everything happens for a reason. This unwavering faith is why I could accomplish the 'impossible' and recover the wealth I spent years accumulating and only four months losing.

My initial response to "Why are you here?" was vague: "To become a self-made millionaire." Years later, I realized that this was neither the reason I was here nor the outcome I desired; it was merely a means to accomplish the desired outcomes. To become a millionaire is a highly equivocal goal; however, when asked, most entrepreneurs will respond similarly, not realizing that it is ambiguous.

The definition of a millionaire is merely having a net worth of one million dollars or more. If that is your goal in life, it is a poor one because a million-dollar net worth doesn't guarantee that you will be wealthy.

Consider Michael Jackson. Michael, a brilliant artist and one of our time's most talented pop icons, spent most of his later years destitute. Although he owned assets worth approximately one billion dollars, he lacked liquid assets and was perpetually in debt. After his passing, Michael left the earth with over $500,000,000 in unpaid debt.

Consider those who won the lottery. Most become overnight millionaires, only to become bankrupt within three to four years. After reading many books on finance, I soon realized that money doesn't make you wealthy and that becoming a millionaire is not the purpose of life. It is, in actuality, not even a goal.

I say that money doesn't make you rich because if you earn three million dollars (a goal many people strive for) and spend five million of those dollars, you are still poor--yes, poor--and exceedingly ignorant regarding financial matters. More money will have no effect. It will worsen the situation.

My definition of a poor person is someone who spends irresponsibly, can't manage his finances, can't defer gratification, spends more than they earn, and blames others for his or her foolishness.

Primarily, a poor person makes poor decisions, notably financial ones. Not particularly a lack of intelligence but a financial intelligence that led to these decisions. You can be brilliant and have inadequate financial management skills.

On the other hand, a wealthy man makes prudent financial decisions, spends less than he or she earns, and invests the difference rather than squandering it on non-essentials.

For instance, I asked an acquaintance a straightforward question: "If you won $1,000,000 in the lottery, what would you do with it?"

My friend responded, "I'll buy a sports car, return to school, and graduate from college, then buy a house for my mother, the best gadgets I can afford, the best clothes, and I'll have every female I've ever lusted after.

I will purchase a mansion in California and spend the first two months on the shore, celebrating my newfound wealth, before investing or saving a portion of it. Oh, and I'll leave my job without a doubt."

Sounds attractive, right? The reality is that most individuals share comparable thought patterns. This is the ideal example of a poor individual with $1,000,000 in his pocket. If you do the math, you will realize that this man will spend his million dollars before graduating from the new college he enrolled in and will end up in massive debt due to a simple lack of financial savvy.

Ask a wealthy individual who is "temporarily broke" the same question, and he or she will respond, "I will invest the money in an asset and let that asset pay for a sports car, a beach vacation, and a house for my mother." In this situation, simplicity is preferable.

Rich people purchase and invest in assets (real estate, businesses, stocks, royalty products, etc.) which then buy stuff for them. As soon as I realized this concept, I changed my response to "I want to become wealthy."

I desired to earn large sums of money and be able to multiply them by two and three, transforming a simple million into five million, ten million into a billion, and so on. Thus, I lived a few years with only one goal: wealth.

At 23, I became wealthy; however, my answer changed once more after making and losing money and spending my money and time with people who did not appreciate me, females who did not care about me, and friends who were not my true friends.

The realization dawned on me that although being wealthy is amazing, being wealthy and lonely is not enjoyable. Being wealthy and ill or being wealthy and despised by everyone was also something I did not desire.

I had to reconsider and reformulate my response, and two years later, after 24 years on planet Earth, I finally understood. The only answer I sought was not to become a millionaire or an affluent person but to become wealthy.

What does it entail to become prosperous?

Well, wealth is abundance, and abundance is love, money, health, happiness, and everything else you require. Abundance is everything you need combined. Abundance was my goal and the only thing I was dedicated to attaining; it was my dream.

Perhaps you already have an abundance of resources, but you lack money. Perhaps your goal is to earn a million dollars, become wealthy, or even a millionaire; that's fine. This book was not written to tell you what you should strive for; doing so would misuse your time and money. I wrote this book to instruct you on attaining your greatest aspiration, whether a million, a billion, or any other quantity of money.

Why, then, am I here?

I was designed to acquire and distribute prosperity. The wealth of money, education, love, happiness, and success will assist me and others in achieving what we desire most, whether it's making more money, decreasing weight, being happier, or starting a business.

I am here to make my own and others' aspirations come true. That is my life's mission; that is why I exist; that is why God decided to position me on Earth.

Why are you here then?

Don't be disheartened if you have not yet discovered the answer to this question. You picked up this book because, like me, you are searching for answers, and the only way to discover them is to continue searching.

You may discover different answers to that question, and it may take you a while to determine which one is best for you, but if you continue searching, you will find the answer to the most important question you can ask yourself.

What   Am   I   Doing   Here?

_____

_____

I would like you to complete the void. Answer this question immediately and write your response in the void on the previous page. Don't worry about the specifics; you can answer this question after the book.

This chapter is about more than just earning money; it is about making a choice, taking a risk, determining the answer to that question, and pursuing your dreams. No hesitation, no second thoughts, just going for it.

Before the end of this chapter, you will realize that if you don't pursue your dreams, you are fighting your creation because you deny what God has given you, which is more essential than anything else in life: your purpose.

Why do you get out of bed in the morning without purpose?

Why will you be working?

Why did you (or will you) have kids?

What are you doing here?

Why does anything happen if you lack a firm sense of life's purpose?

The only significant difference between humans and animals is the ability to be self-aware and go beyond merely surviving and accomplishing something. I'm not simply referring to earning money or losing weight; I'm referring to a sense of purpose, something greater than yourself. Existing for the sake of existing is a fearful goal.

If you have a passion for real estate investing and aspire to become a real estate mogul, your purpose may be to change the appearance of your favored city, make life more affordable, or improve the lives of the people there. Donald J. Trump also desired to make a statement by changing the skyline of New York City.

If you have a passion for computers, your goal is to become a wealthy software programmer and create a virtual world where people worldwide will be given another chance at life, then build software and establish an empire.

Bill Gates, the founder of Microsoft, and Mark Zuckerberg, the founder of Facebook, made comparable decisions. Bill Gates's mission made him the world's richest man then: to serve as the interface between man and machine for every computer sold worldwide. Everything worked out flawlessly.

It is acceptable if your aspirations are not business-related or world-changing. Consider Mother Teresa. Her mission was to assist those who lacked resources and could not care for themselves.

The Dali Lama's mission is to raise enough money and influence enough people so Tibet can be a free nation again. What a forceful declaration! Every week, the NY1 Channel announces the New Yorker of the Week, who is always a person with a mission.

They are not billionaires, millionaires, or individuals who change the universe's appearance; they have changed their lives and those around them because they have a strong sense of purpose. These men will never appear on a suicide list.

You don't need to be Bill Gates, Mother Teresa, Robert Kiyosaki, Henry Ford, Quentin Tarantino, Robert De Niro, or the president of the United States to change the world, nor do you need a billion-dollar dream, a life-changing goal, or a greater-than-life purpose.

"To be the happiest man or woman I can be"; "To be the first woman executive in my company"; "To create the best environment for my child to grow up in"; "To become one of Hollywood's best directors," etc.

You only need a dream, a goal so ambitious that your pulse begins to race whenever you consider it. This is a divine gift; desire derives from "From The Father." It will be your greatest regret at the end of your life if you ignore your talent and don't attempt to achieve your goals because you are unwilling to take risks or believe a family member would disapprove. This will eventually lead to mediocrity, your greatest source of regret.

No book will miraculously make you a millionaire overnight, including this one. Because there are no secret formulas for prosperity, it will not teach you any. Building a business, selling a product, or investing in income-generating assets or products, such as real estate, toys, paper assets, TV repair, deodorants, or potable water, can lead to financial success.

It's no secret that to shed some weight, you must exercise and consume properly, that to be happy, you must rid yourself of negative thoughts and be healthy and healthily use your body and mind.

Many books, seminars, self-help experts, and preachers teach you how to achieve these goals, but haven't you already read them? It would be best to read the "How to Get Rich" book, which teaches how to establish a business and invest in real estate. Did you not peruse the book "How to Lose Weight" that instructs you on better caring for your body? Do you not realize smoking cigarettes will harm you?

You do, but you take no action in response. Perhaps you want to, but you can't bring yourself to act. Perhaps you have already tried but without success. Perhaps you are getting results but wish to take the next step. I believe this book can assist you regardless of your situation.

This chapter is about recognizing your most audacious goals and doing whatever it takes to achieve them. Similar to accumulating a fortune, this will be the most difficult task ever.

If you want to remain in your current position, I advise you not to read this book; it will only confuse you and may cause you to take risks you would otherwise avoid, and your attorney will send me a furious email threatening to sue me because I ruined your life.

Therefore, if you are joyful, fulfilled, full of joy and abundance, I salute you, but I also recommend that you give this book to a friend or someone unhappy, but I must warn you. If you choose to read this book and follow my advice, you will experience temporary unhappiness. I can virtually guarantee it.

This is actuality. Anything truly worthwhile will not be as simple as you believe it to be and will likely cause you stress and suffering in the first few months before you can reap the rewards.

Starting a business from nothing is easy; making it a success is hard; deciding to be an actor and moving to California is easy; living in the back of your truck with no money to eat without going home to cry to mommy is hard; deciding to overcome people's judgments of you and climb the corporate ladder to become the first female executive of a billion dollar company is easy, actually doing it is a completely different story; sketching a skyscraper in Manhattan is easy, actually building.

So, if you want a fast fix, buy a "get rich quick" book or a "magic pill" and see how that works out, but if you decide to follow the advice in this chapter, you will experience frustration, unhappiness, and the desire to resign. Your livelihood depends on it.

However, when you achieve it, reach the pinnacle, and have mastered the process, you will be more than pleased and fulfilled. You will discover a new world and a new you while pursuing your ambitions, and you can't believe you did not do so sooner.

This is not the advice you were expecting to find in a book about building wealth and realizing your dreams, but do you want an author to sell you rosy tales about how beautiful and straightforward the process is?

Or would you rather hear the truth?

This is life and real-life advice: if you are satisfied with your life, finances, and weight, you will not take any action to change your life, but comfort is the worst possible place to be.

Frustration is the only human emotion that can help more people become millionaires, lose weight, and realize their most desired ambitions. Yes, frustration is the most effective motivator; if you know how to use it, refine it, and transform it into motivation, it will be the necessary fuel to propel you toward your goal.

If you can't comprehend it, it will give you a heart attack and cause you other frustration. In this book, you will also discover how frustration can be used to create the 'you' you desire and how to use it to propel yourself toward achieving your ambitions, regardless of their nature.

As previously stated, frustration is only the beginning; you will need to start the business, write the plan, invest the time to make it a reality, manage it, and close your first transaction, which will not be simple. It will be difficult for you to acquire your tenth client while feeling frustrated.

It will not be easy to go from earning $400 per month to $4,000 per month; it will not be easy to manage the money; it will not be easy to deal with angry clients; it will not be easy to handle a lawsuit; it will not be easy to meet deadlines and combat stress; it will not be easy to convince banks and raise money from investors; however, if you understand your purpose, you can enjoy the process.

If you can truly answer the question above, it will not be as bad; even if you lose the business, gain the weight back, lose the big client, get rejected by agents and have the door slammed in your face, become homeless, or suffer a defeat, it will not be the end of the world.

You will succeed as long as you get up the next day and attempt again, as long as you don't give up, as long as you remain focused, and as long as you learn to use your frustration to propel you forward if you allow it to fuel you and propel you forward after all-you can't fail if you never resign.

Donald Trump, one of my heroes, is an excellent example. In the early 1990s, he was perilously nearly bankrupt, with over eight billion dollars in business debt and over nine hundred million dollars in personal guarantees. Trump's days were numbered; newspapers published negative articles about him, and the media presented the 'fact' that he would never ascend again.

Trump negotiated with the banks, slept three hours per night, fought, remained optimistic, and did what no one else would have done. He even convinced the banks that he was too large to fail, and despite the debt and problems, he was able to secure another sixty million dollars to save his empire. Today, he is still among the world's wealthiest individuals; this is just one example.

You might not like or adore Trump as much as I do; if so, consider Tim Blixseth, who refused to resign after declaring bankruptcy. Today, his net worth exceeds one billion dollars. Consider Steve Jobs, who suffered from a severe case of depression after being fired from Apple in 1985, or David Murdock, who nearly lost everything in the 2008 real estate collapse.

Stephen Ross is a brilliant real estate developer who was on the verge of bankruptcy in the early 1990s and went on to create a sixteen-billion-dollar empire in less than four years. T. Boone Pickens is a brilliant billionaire who had to start over after losing everything when oil and gas prices crashed.

What would you do if you got a phone call from the bank tomorrow informing you that you owe $900,000,000? Seriously, you would flee.

Would you commit suicide?

Would you seek employment and attempt to repay it?

What if you were a parent with three small children?

What if, amidst the chaos, your wife files for divorce and decides to prosecute you for everything?

Can you withstand that level of pressure?

Can you deal with such stress?

As previously stated, I make no promises that this chapter will change your life, nor can I guarantee that your life will change immediately.

I can only hope to educate you and help you better understand the process of going against the odds to achieve what you want, how not to quit and hold on when everything around you seems to be collapsing, how to identify what you want and get it; how to handle enormous amounts of pressure and stress; how to swim against the current when everyone is saying "no!"; how to ignore the comments of sarcastic friends, unsupportive spouses, and disappointed fat people.

Yes, I accomplished my goal of acquiring prosperity. I am wealthy, healthy, happy, and successful and I have shed a few pounds. Yes, I still have a long distance to reach my desired destination. I do hope, however, that you will heed some of my advice and join me on this journey toward achieving your ambition, whatever it may be.

If you follow my recommendation and pursue your ambitions, you must realize you will no longer be in the "Safe Zone." When you make that decision, you will enter the jungle of life.

For a lion cub who grew up in a menagerie, moving into the jungle is a terrifying experience; the likelihood of failure is high. You can lose everything but are determined if you work hard and refuse to let your fear of failure control your life. If you enjoy what you do with DEDICATION, you will succeed! Winners and losers are differentiated by their capacity for action.

CHAPTER 2: ARE YOU A PERSON WITH DEDICATED GOALS?

Consider yourself a goal-oriented individual. You feel lost if you don't constantly strive for something, so you must be the sort of person who must constantly pursue something. If so, congratulations; most individuals are not goal oriented. You can learn how to become goal-oriented if you are not already one.

A goal-oriented individual is always successful in life. They have a rigid outlook on what they wish to accomplish and acquire. They are extremely intelligent individuals who are always willing to take the necessary risks to achieve their goals.

Anyone can set a goal; it is not difficult to do so. However, what is more important is having the perseverance to attain the goal. It requires effort, dedication, conviction, and courage. It would be best to recognize that you will not achieve your goals immediately; reaching them may take considerable time.

They realize that they must have reasonable timelines to achieve their goals. The problem with most individuals is that they demand immediate gratification. If something doesn't happen when they expect it to, they become frustrated and give up on their goals.

A goal-oriented person recognizes this and has learned how to cultivate the burning desire necessary to achieve their goals. However, when things take a while, they may veer off course. They comprehend that it is acceptable and always get back on course.

Can you claim that this is your approach to achieving your goals?

You can acquire the skills necessary to achieve your goals in life. However, it all begins with a burning desire to attain a specific goal. Without motivation, it is impossible to achieve your goals.

Ultimately, pursuing your aspirations can be somewhat dangerous. You must overcome your fear of failure and realize you can accomplish what you want. They recognize that they must establish attainable goals to achieve success. Can you visualize yourself achieving your goals?

There is no distinction between successful and unsuccessful individuals, except that successful individuals are always motivated to achieve their goals.

Then why are you still waiting?

They are just around the corner if you are willing to take small measures toward your goals. Why not start now and be grateful for what you did rather than continue to make excuses not to start and regret not having the courage to pursue your dreams?

If you take the first step, you will discover it is not as hard as some think. You will regain your zest for life when you realize that you can achieve anything you set your mind to, and you will instill this belief in your offspring.

Remember that when you were a teenager, you believed everyone was gazing at every flaw you had. Thankfully, as we age, we realize that most people aren't all concerned with our actions. However, I often encounter job applicants who appear stuck in the mindset that "Everyone is looking at me!"

Few things are flawless, and most people don't have "perfect" resumes. We work with many clients with employment gaps, career transitions, short-lived positions, and other obstacles. They also possess extensive experience, a diligent work ethic, and a strong desire to succeed. Which of these do you believe employers value the most?

Certain career obstacles can't be overcome. For instance, if you have a nursing degree, you can't work as a barrister. You will not be recruited as CEO if your resume contains only two years of work experience. However, many of the concerns that job seekers have with their resumes are of little concern to those reviewing them.

Hiring managers understand if you took time off to care for your children or ailing parents, particularly if you maintained your professional certifications and have since returned to work. They also recognize that sometimes you accept a position with a company that goes out of business within a year, leaving you unemployed.

As you seek a position, your primary responsibility is to market one product: yourself! As your parents advised you as an adolescent, it's time to stop dwelling on your flaws and concentrate on the positive qualities you can offer an employer.

If you want the person who will hire you to focus on your abilities, you must maintain a positive attitude. Regarding professional flaws, it is best to recognize them, acknowledge them, and move on.

CHAPTER 3: WHAT DO YOU BELIEVE, WHERE DO YOU STAND AND HOW ARE YOU DOING?

If you want to live a meaningful existence, you must reflect on the things that are significant to you and act accordingly with true dedication. This applies to both your professional and personal lives.

Occasionally, set pen to paper (or fingers to keyboard) to record your beliefs and values in granular detail. Periodically, add, subtract, and clarify as feedback from your life dictates. Implement the "lousy feeling in the pit of your stomach" test as a check-in.

When you're feeling terrible - I mean bad - because of an action you've taken or a result in your life, you should ask yourself, "Which of the beliefs or values I espouse am I violating?" The response to this question will assist you in gaining clarity and reinforcing or refining your perspective.

Never lower your standards to accommodate your frailty as a human being.

Never come up with excuses or rationalize poor performance.

Never compromise your aspirations. Instead, up your game to get closer to your goals and move your life away from your fears and toward your finest performance!

I've pondered this topic extensively. The following is a condensed account of my guiding beliefs and values:

I've never been content with "sending in" my existence or living on autopilot. I have clear beliefs regarding what I wish to stand for. I consistently fall short, but that is beside the point. The point is that few things in life are significant. Those few do matter tremendously.

Most people lament the perceived wrongs they believe the world has committed against them or how things should be but aren't. They don't devote sufficient energy to "appearing" in the world as they would like - no excuses.

Since it explains the world in terms of what we owe it rather than what it owes us, this information is neither trendy nor popular. It rejects victimhood in favor of individual responsibility. We must stand for something, or else we will do almost anything.

I believe in integrity, loyalty, honesty, courage and bravery, accountability for actions and outcomes, discipline, and perseverance, even though I have repeatedly failed.

I had to seek out alternative role models for the last two items because I grew up in a household where these traits were not prevalent. The virtues I espouse are, in reality, all aspirations, as I fall short of my standards in every area.

However, when I am assessed, I use these characteristics as checkpoints. Consequently, I often make decisions that don't feel right at the time because doing the right thing isn't always easy or enjoyable, but I usually look back and conclude I made a decent choice.

Most people fill their lives with people who pity them, over-sympathize, and validate them; they pat them on the head and say, "There, you did the best you could. The problem is the universe, not you." They then make the same ineffective judgments and repeatedly take the same ineffective actions.

They gain no wisdom and remain stagnant. They are in the same position as cavemen from 5,000 years ago who dragged their knuckles across the ground and carved enigmatic symbols on the walls of their dwellings.

I believe in encircling myself with people who will serve as a model for me, as opposed to those who will exacerbate my flaws through their own ineffective behavior or useless validation. I want to surround myself with individuals who push me to excel and applaud my efforts.

Similarly, many of us, including myself, more often than I care to acknowledge, choose friends, business associates, spouses, or significant others who provide only cowardly feedback.

These well-intentioned enablers make us feel positive about our current situation. I believe that genuine, true, courageous friends prioritize telling the truth over maintaining peace. They prioritize the welfare of their peers over the continuation of cozy friendships.

While problem-solving or the aftermath of an event, I often ask myself, "What lesson is life trying to teach me right now?" Often, the initial, most obvious response to a question is not the actual response, and I must dig deeper or wait.

Occasionally, the lesson takes years to percolate and surface, so it is often too late to address the issue that prompted it. My forbearance is not synchronized with the calendar that life uses to cultivate my wisdom.

In a recent reference letter that one of my CEO clients wrote about me to a colleague at another company, he stated, "When Rand opens his mouth, the truth comes out." This is the highest compliment I've ever received.

I believe in pursuing the truth, even if it leads me to extremely unpleasant locations. Often, MY truth represents reality as I would like it to be rather than reality as it is, and I must change it to accommodate the truth. I detest it when that happens!

I want my existence to have meaning. I am not speaking romantically. John Gardner once said, "In my experience, it is a rare person who can go through life like a stray cat, taking pleasures where they can and passing unnoticed." In my existence, I wish for the whole to exceed the sum of its parts. I desire a resounding crescendo that I can be pleased with.

I believe that personal development should be our primary, lifelong goal. Especially in later years, it becomes simple to become imprisoned by attitudes, preconceptions, and resentments that have outlived their usefulness. We can remain vigorous, curious, and adaptable for as long as we live, albeit with increased rigor and tenacity as we age.

Once, it was said, "Life is the art of drawing without an eraser." We can't undo our past actions, but we can improve our future performance. Rarely but occasionally, when we're extremely fortunate, we get a "do-over." This is God's second opportunity, and we must not squander it.

I believe in the strength of knowledge. Experience imparts wisdom, but not always. There is a significant difference between ten years of experience and one year of experience multiplied ten times.

For experience to result in enlightenment, reflection, discernment, and permanent behavioral modifications must follow. Our culture has given "judgment" a negative reputation in recent years.

Although we are reminded not to be judgmental, the most successful individuals constantly judge. We judge when deciding whether to embrace a job opportunity. We judge when we select our companions. When we choose to drive to the office instead of utilizing public transportation on a given day, we judge. We judge when we choose to forgive someone who has harmed us.

Judgment leads to persecution.

When it stems from a position of certainty.

When it fosters our moral superiority, it is destructive.

When it informs our productive spiritual evolution.

When it promotes personal development - it is advantageous and can impart wisdom.

I believe that the dedications we make and maintain shape and reveal our character. I'm not talking about our focus on goal setting and accomplishment, although those are essential components of dedication. I am referring to the disposition to maintain our word reliably and carefully.

When we make a promise or give our word, we should regard it as a sacred trust, regardless of the magnitude or nature of the dedication. When we commit to doing something, we should follow through. Every time we say we will be somewhere, we should be there! In our culture, vows are regarded as arbitrary promises rarely honored.

I believe it's never too late to discover happiness and that it's well worth the effort. One of life's greatest challenges, if not THE greatest, is determining which bridges to cross and which ones to fire to achieve a goal without causing undue harm to others.

I have, at times, considered honor and contentment to be mutually exclusive. I've interpreted honor as "doing the right thing" and pleasure as "doing the pleasurable thing," and have felt morally superior for choosing one path and excessively guilty for choosing the other.

Neither option is advantageous; I have been a slow learner with excessively rigid boundaries. In contrast, when these two alternatives present an irreconcilable dichotomy that legitimately requires a choice, I find that choosing honor over happiness is more ennobling, even if it's not as viscerally or instantaneously satisfying. It has taken over 60 years to learn this lesson.

I've always been someone others can depend on, and I enjoy that. I have often been the hero who arrives on a white steed to save the day. In a foxhole, when disaster strikes, I've been a "go-to guy." I desire the ball after the game and am unafraid to take the final, decisive shot.

I am thankful that I am significantly better at this now than a decade or two or three ago. However, I am still a work in progress. As I get older, I discover that my character and reputation are the things I value the most. Through the agony of personal transgressions, I've learned that they are always easier to protect and defend than to regain once lost.

Now you know who I am! What are YOUR beliefs, where are YOUR positions, and how are YOU doing?

CHAPTER 4: ARE YOU SUCCESSFUL OR ARE YOU SIMPLY CHASING YOUR TAIL?

We discuss accomplishment as if it were an event or a thing. People are referred to as donning "the badges of success" and carrying (or wearing or driving) the most recent status symbol.

But success is a manner of being in the world, not an object.

If you are not pursuing your life's genuine purpose, you can have all the wealth in the world and still feel like a failure. This is a unique type of tension.

Or, if you follow your passion, you may have nothing but the clothes on your back and feel like the greatest success in the world. This is a very unique form of 'Bliss.'

Daily, you may slog through your to-do list or Goals Project Plan, cross off most of the major tasks, and feel like you've had a productive day.

Are you, however, barking up the incorrect tree?

By following your heart, a completed task is meaningless if it doesn't bring you closer to your true-life goals.

Therefore, what does it mean to follow one's heart?

One way to consider this is to inquire, "From whom do I receive approval? Is it coming from within me or from others?"

"Where do I find fulfillment?

Do I find it in objects and other people or my solitude?"

These are difficult issues. Perhaps you can't even recall a time when you experienced inner silence. That may be because you are pursuing too many noisy objects.

There is nothing 'deadly serious' about the pursuit of interior silence. It leads to increased enjoyment. More pleasure, not depression or fatigue, increases effectiveness because the strength gained from inner silence restores one's capacity to recognize what is genuinely valuable: friendship, affection, compassion, and dedication to a cause greater than oneself.

If it's not too melancholy, picture yourself on your deathbed.

What will you consider the highlights of your life?

When did you realize that you are the only measure for success and failure?

Achievement is not an event. Success is a mental state.

Victor Frankl should have the final word on accomplishment. As a prisoner in Nazi concentration centers, Victor Frankl developed his theories and methods as a psychotherapist of the highest caliber.

"Success, like happiness, can't be pursued; it must happen as an unachieved byproduct of one's dedication to a cause greater than oneself."

Are we merely mortal, correct?

No wonder many people fixate on the negative and become depressed. When you switch on the television in the morning, you are immediately bombarded with depressing news and events. Wouldn't it be nice if there was a channel dedicated to "happy thoughts"?

Unfortunately, positive emotions are not what sells advertising. How can one prevent these negative emotions from dominating one's subconscious? Throw away your old television and stop paying your cable bill. I guarantee that you will immediately observe an improvement in your overall demeanor.

Okay, so most of us wouldn't go that far, but how about a game of mind control and how we cope with or react to the constant barrage of negative stimuli? You alone can control how you respond to negative thoughts and determine whether you are a cheerful camper or a sad puppy.

The most crucial factor in determining whether you have a happy core is how you process the negatives presented to you; do you dwell on these negatives and allow them to stew in your mind, or can you discard them quickly?

You have won the war if you can master the ability to process and filter out disagreeable negative information in your mind. Negative individuals tend to dwell on the depressing aspects of their lives and always find someone else to blame for their depressed state.

Positive individuals, on the other hand, learn to process and filter out these negative thoughts and emotions to focus on the positive aspects of their lives. Remember, we live in a world where violence and social unrest are rising, so we must learn to become more optimistic.

I've learned over my forty-plus years that when I start to feel sorry for myself, I think of all the unfortunate people with a feared disease or the person I know who just went through a nasty, acrimonious divorce. I must remind myself that my life is good and I have no reason to feel miserable.

In conclusion, you will be much happier if you can concentrate on daily blessings and positive things in your life! We are all human, and negative thoughts will continue to bombard us, but how we respond to them will determine whether we conclude the day as a happy camper or a sad, terrified puppy.

CHAPTER 5: HOW DEDICATED ARE YOU TO THE DESIRES YOU EXPRESS?

I want to share an anecdote with you as I embark on my marriage week. My partner and I have been living together for twelve years, so I know a bit or two about dedication. I can now state that I am truly dedicated, and I feel great about that. I'll reveal a secret about overcoming your fear of dedication and embracing everything that comes with it shortly.

Let's first examine some definitions of devotion.

I discovered some examples online at The Free Dictionary and vocabulary.com.

a. Referral to the committee of a legislative measure. (Okay, we'll disregard that because we're discussing intimate relationships here.)

b. Official delivery, such as to a penitentiary or mental health facility. (believe it or not, many individuals believe this, which is why they are not in a dedicated relationship!)

c. A promise, specifically a contractual obligation involving a financial obligation. (Are you all set?)

d. The condition of being emotionally or intellectually bound to a course of action or another individual or individuals:

e. committing or pledging (you can perform the action but not experience it; sometimes, this method works!)

f. the condition of being dedicated (Do your actions reflect your state of being?)

g. a dedication that restricts one's freedom of action (What?)

h. entails committing to something, such as a person or a cause. Before making a dedication, you should consider it carefully. A dedication binds you to do something.

When my companion and I began dating 12 years ago, I was terrified of committing.

Three years had passed since I emerged from my near-marriage experience. I was engaged to a decent man, but my life circumstances and lack of relationship awareness led to its demise. He was present with me during my father's assassination of my mother. In some respects, he was my salvation until he was no longer my salvation.

It was time for me to examine my patterns of self-abuse, codependence, and lack of accountability in detail. I can't do that while in that relationship. I did not know where his unconscious patterns began, and mine ended, and in retrospect, the relationship had to end so I could develop.

After what had transpired with my parents, I did not trust anyone. My energy vibration plummeted, and I began attracting companions similarly victimized by their lives and stories. That is until the day I realized I needed to change.

Perhaps it was my secret compulsive eating or my excessive exercise that occasionally led to injuries. It was my derriere that ultimately awoke me. For you, it may be prescription drug abuse, excessive alcohol consumption, or excessive Internet use with strangers. Take a goal look at yourself.

I awoke enough to scrap my friendships and relationships with those who identified as victims and pursued a degree in Spiritual Psychology, where I learned how to work more positively with the cards I was dealt. I accomplished this by accepting full responsibility and being kind to myself throughout the process.

I was counseled for two years and learned how to counsel myself and others. I learned how to listen to others and myself with empathy. As I rebuilt my relationship with myself, my heart expanded again.

I met Roseline, who would later become my life partner during this period. She was a graduate of the identical curriculum. I met Roseline because I promised not to seek a partner who would complete me or compensate me for the qualities I lacked. Moreover, these relationships often cause you to continue living in a place of inferiority.

Instead, I desired a partner who possessed the qualities I most admired in myself.

We gathered, and it was a magical occasion. Immediate attraction, affectionate respect, and happiness. Amazing, right?

I've struck a brick wall. Many months into the relationship, she asked me if I wanted to commit, prompting me to spill my tea at the restaurant where we were dining. I believe my knee also kicked the table.

I believe the waiter fell and poured water on Roseline's lap. No serious! My first words were, "Is dedication similar to being dedicated to a mental hospital? Why would I want to do that?

What?!

I enjoy such occasions immensely. My response was so outsized and inappropriate that it had nothing to do with her. When I considered devotion, I recalled my parents' thirty-year marriage, which ended in betrayal and murder. No surprise, I felt fearful. No wonder I had avoided relationships with decent individuals for years. I was uninterested if they were excessively attentive, kind, and available.

Or what about the emotionally unavailable individuals I was attracted to?

I received a wake-up call. I was attracted to them due to my emotional inaccessibility. I'd sell my emotions for a dime. In actuality, their lack of dedication was to my liking. All of this was unconscious at the time.

How about looking at your life and determining who reflects something about you to you? I do not doubt that you will have some profound insights.

I did my interior work and overcame that inner obstacle before dedicating myself to my lovely girlfriend. This was made possible by my devotion to love. Choosing to be in a relationship with her was the first step in gaining confidence in my ability to make loving decisions.

Relationships require effort because we are all unique. This difference keeps things interesting, but it can also present difficulties. Anyone in a long-term, healthy relationship knows that communication, dedication, and respect are the three most important factors in maintaining the relationship. Occasionally, one will be sufficient to carry you through difficult circumstances.

Therefore, if you are ready for a dedicated relationship, dig deep and genuinely commit to loving.

Start by committing to

* Be someone someone else would want to commit to

*Get in shape

*Eat properly so you have the energy

*Get help with any addictions you may have

*Take care of yourself *Get your hair done *Iron your clothes.

Commit yourself to leaving your comfort zone.

* Listen to others with your heart

*Be flexible

*Dedicate yourself to a long-term relationship if you discover someone special

*Commit to loyalty

After making these decisions, the necessary actions will naturally follow.

How can you overcome your apprehension of dedication and embrace it so that your words and actions align?

Do your inner task! To heal your latent patterns, you must bring them into conscious awareness.

What could be better than creating a life with someone and having them as your partner?

CHAPTER 6: ARE YOU SATISFIED WITH YOUR CURRENT LIFESTYLE?

When you reach the end of your brief physical existence, will you wish you had spent more time pursuing wealth, or would you rather have invested your most valuable resource, namely your time, in cultivating meaningful relationships?

In reality, we are so driven to meet society's expectations, to amass as many resources as possible, and to attain as much power or fame as possible that we neglect what truly matters, namely family and true companions.

Will you continue wasting your life on something that will have little significance for you?

Or will you change your life and pursue the things that truly matter and will make you joyful and fulfilled?

When you prioritize pleasure and fulfillment over money, you can live a full and meaningful life, and money also seems to flow toward you almost effortlessly. Change your motivations; pursue what truly matters to you, and you will live an extraordinary, full, and abundant existence.

Develop relationships with influential individuals.

Relationships with family and acquaintances must be actively nurtured, much like a beautiful garden of flowers. Creating and maintaining strong relationships requires time, effort, and creativity. The greater the effort's quality, sincerity, and consistency, the more likely the relationship will flourish and develop. Life's greatest value derives from caring for and sharing one's existence with significant others.

Give the Gift of Your Continual Development to Those Around You Invest time in your ongoing development. As you grow, you can contribute greater value to everyone you influence. When forming relationships that will give your life meaning and contribute to your satisfaction, giving them the gift of your consistent dedication to personal growth and development is prudent.

Develop into Someone of Worth.

You can give anyone this wonderful gift because you become a more valuable friend or family member as you mature and develop. You increase the value of the relationship. I believe in the adage, "I will take the best care of myself, and you should take the best care of yourself so that we are both better people who can take better care of each other."

Stop allowing yourself to conceal behind the phony walls you've constructed, the barriers that convince you that you must pursue wealth before discovering contentment. Whatever you seek will always evade you.

You are trapped in mediocrity by the barriers you believe will protect you from the unhappiness your current circumstances are causing you. You will remain in your comfort zone until you break down these artificial boundaries you erected to prevent anything from entering your self-imposed comfort zone.

An artificial barrier will always prevent you from reaching your full potential, block the happiness you deserve, and prevent the flow of the money you desire. You will continue to live a life devoid of fulfillment and purpose.

Allow yourself to begin to soar toward your pleasure and limitless potential immediately by severing all ties. All that is required is a small shift in your perspective and actions, and you will almost immediately begin to experience the most astounding things in your life.

You have much to gain and nothing to lose but frustration and discontent. Pull the trigger and unleash your true, authentic self; permit yourself to become the person of your desires.

CHAPTER 7: ARE YOU READY TO BE DEDICATED?

We will not have a final moment, correct? That only happens to other individuals. Well, it could happen at any time, maybe today or next week, but according to statistics, we have so many years left, so why worry? When it arrives, it arrives.

Why bother?

You can't change the final instant. You can't justify it by claiming it is irrelevant. It is true. I have been with people as they passed away, and I can say that their final moments can be either traumatic or peaceful, depending on how they led their lives.

Death-approaching visions can be terrifying, with the individual struggling to sit up and flee away or incredibly peaceful, uttering, "I see beautiful people, wonderful gardens, and I hear beautiful music."

Are you straightforward with your relationships right now?

Is there anything that you feel compelled to complete?

Are you extremely attached to belongings like your residence that will tug at your heart in that final moment?

Can you let go of every loved one? Have you considered these matters?

Your financial affairs should be in order.

Is your spouse ready to assume leadership?

Do you currently possess more than you require?

Can you assist those in need of necessities?

All these things are essential in that final instant when time condenses, and you can view your entire existence instantly. The ego's bias is then rendered powerless, and the view of your life is viewed through uncolored lenses.

There must be no misgivings, last-minute adjustments, or loose ends in the final moment. Have you lived a blameless existence, or has everything been about you?

Did you have room for your family, acquaintances, and the less fortunate? If not, then why? Unless now, when? This is also essential at the last minute.

Have you prepared your mind so that you will not fear pain when your time arrives?

Have you experimented with and conquered pain, or do you rush to the medicine cabinet or doctor at the first sign of discomfort?

Will there be no solitude in the final instant?

No aversion to the unknown? No?

Then what have you been doing with your existence if you have only been having fun and entertaining yourself as if you were immortal? This is all extremely vital and will determine whether you die with courage or great fear.

You can't delay until the last minute to complete everything. If you are unprepared, you will only experience mass confusion and despair at the end, when you realize that there is no escape this time and you are certain to die soon. This is not the behavior of a combatant; it is unbecoming of anyone. This fearful apprehension doesn't augur well for your transition into your next existence.

How you leave matters tremendously. Will fervent prayer compensate for a lifetime of selfishness and change your destiny? Do your actions matter, or can you do whatever you want and still be saved? You will discover the truth when your final moment happens.

Your final moment is a compression, the sum and substance of a brief lifetime, a burst of lightning. You can no longer spin your existence; it is what it is, and one can no longer deceive oneself. That's it. This is your identity.

If we could see this incredible final moment while we were still healthy and alive, we would sell everything and give it to people experiencing poverty, dedicating our lives to helping others as Jesus instructed so that we have no baggage, attachments, and regrets when the time comes. Few, however, comprehend this, living their lives without any awareness.

Therefore, don't delay any further. Life is comparable to a bubble in a stream that can explode anytime. You could confront your final moment next week or next month.

When we don't confront our last moment, put it off, and believe we have plenty of time, we become careless about life, get involved in trivial things that don't matter in our last moment, and even harm others for our selfish pleasure. We become irresponsible and overconfident, referred to as ignorance and delusion.

Amazingly, a life lived in abject poverty by choice and devoted to serving others becomes a joy unrivaled by any pleasures we can imagine, a release, a relief, and a life so full that we marvel how we ever managed to do the things we did before. It's a fact. It was Jesus' teaching.

What Are Your Fears?

Do you believe that anxiety could determine whether or not you succeed in a particular endeavor?

I contend that it is not just a possibility but also a probability. More "traditional" obstacles may stand in your way, but this is often an illusion and is not why people fail to achieve their ambitions.

One of the reasons why fear is not seen as the perpetrator is that we typically associate fear with apprehension of failure. However, fear of SUCCESS is often at least as significant a factor.

Let's examine a few instances to illustrate this point.

Are you more terrified of failure or success when losing weight and getting in shape?

The fear of failure appears to be quite evident. You fear that you will not be successful because you have attempted many times in the past without achieving the desired results. You may also fear that you lack the appropriate training or supervision to create health improvements effectively or will sustain an injury.

These are all prevalent concerns regarding physical fitness, but what about the fear of what your success would entail? You would be required to exercise daily, if not every day.

You would need to consume healthy foods and meticulously monitor the types and quantities of foods you consume each day. You would have to devote at least an hour per day to daily exercise and healthy food preparation. You would need to have a long-term dedication to your fitness program and adhere to it.

That sounds like a tremendous amount of labor and very little play! Success in your efforts to lose weight or improve your health sounds like something you may be afraid to undertake for fear of giving up the activities you enjoy.

What about financial autonomy?

Do you believe that fear of success could play a role in that aspect of your life?
Most people fear failure in this regard for traditional reasons: their job doesn't pay enough, they have too many expenses to save a significant amount of money, they don't have enough time to earn extra income, etc.

Again, these concerns may be valid, but what about the fear of success? If you were financially prosperous, you would be saddled with many obligations! Taxes that cost a lot of money are undoubtedly on the list of things that may inspire fear.

Financial success may be a source of distress for you due to the management of your successful business venture. Leaving the "comfort zone" you have always known is undoubtedly terrifying! You may be destitute, but at least you know where you stand, correct?

Again, the anxiety of having to do what it takes to Succeed may be preventing you from sincerely trying to get the money you believe you so desperately desire!

And lastly, let's discuss relationships. Who hasn't feared a relationship's prospective outcome at some point?

On the one hand, the fear of failure is present. You fear that the "one" individual for you doesn't exist. You may fear rejection because you are insufficiently attractive, prosperous, or entertaining. Perhaps you fear that no one will want you because you have a disability, children from a previous marriage, or a chronic condition that you believe discourages others from approaching you.

Those are undeniably formidable concerns, but let's examine the fear of actually succeeding in a long-term relationship:

You may fear "settling down" with one person and giving up the freedom to date others or spend time with those who pique your interest. You may fear being required to be responsible daily once you often interact with another individual or that individual's offspring.

Likewise, you may fear that you will have to give up some of the attention your children give you or that you will have to share responsibility for them with someone else. You may hesitate to enter a long-term relationship because you must start informing your partner about your activities and whereabouts.

Whether referring to a fear of successful health or weight loss, a fear of actually making the kind of money you desire or a fear of the potential outcome of a genuinely successful long-term relationship, one thing is crystal clear: YOU need to get clear!

What will happen if you don't overcome the anxieties that prevent you from achieving success? You will never be! Your fears will keep you precisely where you are today, and in 30 or 40 years, you will still not have any of the things you were too afraid to pursue successfully.

Fear should not hold you back, whether the fear of failure or success. Please determine what you desire, then go out and make it happen. You'll be pleased that you did it in the end!

CHAPTER 8: ARE YOU REALIZING YOUR CAPABILITIES WITH DEDICATION?

Ask the average person if they are reaching their utmost potential, and I'm willing to bet that most of the time, the answer will be no. Ask them if their life would be better if they realized more of their potential, and I'm confident they would almost always say yes.

Why is there a disparity?

Is it a Lack of faith or self-confidence?

Is it a lack of conviction and motivation?

Or, could it be a mindset of contentment with what is acceptable despite the other effort, dedication, or fortitude required to reach for more and use more of their God-given talent and right to do more with their life?

I've read scores of books on maximizing potential, and the common theme in all of them is that we could all accomplish more with our lives. If this is true, why do so few individuals push their limits, strive for more, and lack the motivation to do so?

The fear of rejection or failure is a significant issue. No one enjoys either of these, but you must risk them to achieve more. The only way to succeed or accomplish more is to attempt, and attempting always carries with it the possibility of error, failure, and lessons to be learned.

The potential is merely what is patiently waiting in the wings of your life, hoping that one day you will believe in it and embrace more of it, whether it be in relationships, a career, or an interest that you have failed to accept or decided to embrace out of fear that it may not work out in the end, so you play it safe.

No matter how limited your time, talent, or resources may appear, playing it safe is not a recipe for attaining excellence or doing more with them.

No one knows how much potential they must achieve, but if you don't attempt, you will never know what you could have accomplished.

Do you agree with this? Indeed, most individuals are.

However, we are fortunate that thousands of individuals have pushed their limits and gone for it over the years.

Progress has been made in medicine, technology, travel, and other aspects of life or society. Consider how drastically different your life would be if so many individuals who have accomplished so much with their potential had instead chosen to settle.

I could provide an endless list, but there are a few: Walt Disney, Steve Jobs, Bill Gates, Thomas Edison, Henry Ford, and Bill Marriott. Thousands of individuals have changed our lives because they were unwilling to settle down. The issue, therefore, remains: by settling, what are you not achieving for your family, employees, clients or, society, or perhaps yourself?

CHAPTER 9: DO YOU FEAR TAKING A LEAP OF FAITH?

So many individuals have a hobby they enjoy in addition to a job they detest. How do you determine if and when your hobby should become your primary source of income?

There are obvious financial answers to this question, and I would never advise someone to risk being unable to pay their expenses if that makes them uncomfortable. This section will focus on the spiritual aspect of preparedness.

I know from experience that if your job doesn't align with your authentic self and you have a passion for something else, you will be miserable until you resolve the issue. For some individuals, pursuing their passion on the side may be sufficient. Still, I continually resent the time spent on my "job" that prevented me from pursuing my genuine passion.

So, how do you know when your spirit is ready to devote yourself fully to your passion?

Do you dislike your work and constantly complain about it?

While at work, do you often consider what you could be doing to advance your passion?

Do you genuinely allow your passion to jeopardize your job?

Do you devote nearly every waking instant outside of work to your passion?

I jeopardized my work by reducing my hours to pursue my passion. I know individuals who bring their passion for working and devote company time to it or who continuously complain about their jobs and perform poorly because they are unhappy.

They are eventually confronted and compelled to pursue their passion full-time or learn to focus while on the "job." Clearly (although they may not recognize it), they are sabotaging their livelihood to pursue their passion. They lack the courage to take the risk, forcing someone else to decide on their behalf.

Please consider the following if you find yourself in this situation. No manager (at least none I know of) desires to dismiss anyone. Most of them lose sleep over it, even when they are doing you a favor.

Don't subject someone else to that by forcing them to make your choice! Either take the risk, or if you remain on the job, turn off your passion while you are there and focus on the job when it is expected. If you can't do so, you must leap of faith.

An acquaintance of mine is a sole proprietor in the alternative health industry. His wife worked in sales and traveled often, and they have two young children. Therefore, it was determined that his wife would remain home and assist him with his business. He accepted the challenge despite a significant pay reduction. He dared to admit that he had made some poor choices, and I believe he is now on the correct path.

However, he has always been combative; his (blue) personality type enjoys a challenge! Similarly, red personalities are risk-takers. Greens and yellows will have the most difficulty with these decisions. Greens are thrifty and concerned with their financial security. Yellows put everyone else before themselves and are afraid of causing harm to their family or former employer.

Most people find it difficult to take the plunge, but if you sense that stirring in your soul, act! Start building your faith and self-confidence and devise a plan to pursue your aspirations at the very least. It is the only path to genuine contentment!

CHAPTER 10: ARE YOU A DRIFT OR A CONSTRUCTOR?

How often do you find yourself at the end of the day pondering where the time went and feeling astonishment at how little you've accomplished? I know I do some days! You set out with a plan, but something distracts you, and before you realize it, the day has passed, and you have only scratched the surface of what you had hoped to accomplish. This can be extremely discouraging.

When your days are hectic, but you feel nothing is getting done, you become a "drifter." You have disorganized your day and strayed from the tasks necessary to continue developing and expanding your business.

We can make as many lists as we want, but that will not be sufficient to complete the duties. We must cease being occupied and become productive. In doing so, we become "builders."

Being a constructor requires discipline. Today, there are more methods than ever to become distracted from our tasks. Typically, we carry our mobile phones to answer a call at a moment's notice, respond to every email as soon as we see it arrive, and allow a quick Internet or Facebook check to consume more than just a few minutes of our day.

You may believe you are working your day purposefully, but when you review how you spent your time, you will realize why the tasks are not being completed. There are gaps in your day that need to be filled for you to remain on purpose and work towards meaningful goals that positively impact your business.

I was unaware of how much my email and mobile phone impacted my day when they were a major distraction. I would answer all incoming calls and continually check my email to "stay on top of things."

But rather than remaining on top of things, I was falling further behind in completing the business-building tasks that were most important to me. I would begin a task, become diverted, and require other time to regain my concentration and become truly productive again.

I was present for others but absent for myself and my business; the results reflected this. My business felt disorganized, and I was continually chasing after things. Upon conclusion of most days, I felt exhausted and overburdened. However, it need not be this way.

Take responsibility for your time and become a constructor with your duties. Control your days instead of allowing them to control you. Plan each day so that you are working towards achieving not only the requirements of your clients but also those of your business.

Focus on what truly matters, eliminate distractions, and focus daily on your goals. When you invest time cultivating your business and achieving your goals, I can guarantee you will see results!

The Next Steps:

Take a few days to conduct a thorough audit of your time usage. Document everything you do during the workweek.

Is there ever a time when you allow distractions to dominate?

How often do you read your email?

Do you answer every contact as soon as it arrives?

Are you conversing with peers, sending text messages, or posting on Facebook?

Develop a keen awareness of the interruptions in your day and take deliberate steps to eliminate them.

If you attempt to complete personal tasks during the workday, you must promptly cease doing so. This becomes a mental juggling act as you switch between work and personal life and rapidly lose concentration.

It is a significant burden not only on your time but also on your mental energy. Establish clear boundaries for your workday and adhere to them. Keep personal duties outside of work hours. Remember that getting things done requires more than just contemplation; it also requires focused action!

CHAPTER 11: HOW DEDICATED ARE YOU TO EXCELLENCE AT WORK?

There is an ancient joke about the dedication required to prepare eggs and bacon for breakfast. The joke goes, "The chicken had to work hard but the pig had to be extremely dedicated!"

How dedicated are you to your work?

How much are you prepared to donate?

Suppose you work in an office where someone often needs to stay late. The day before, it was your turn and you stayed. Today is Sally's turn but she had to depart early due to her sick child being sent home from school. Today, your supervisor asks you to remain. You have no real intentions immediately following work.

Do you consent to stay or dispute that you stayed the night before?

Do you have any other colleagues who should remain?

Do you attempt to negotiate with your boss?

Occasionally, employees anticipate more dedication from their employer than they are willing to provide themselves.

What constitutes dedication?

You don't need to work longer and tougher hours as an employee to demonstrate your dedication. In all honesty, you are not required to be devoted to your employer or current position. You only need to be dedicated to yourself and put forth your best effort.

You must conduct a rapid self-evaluation to be fully dedicated to putting forth your best effort. This can be achieved by answering the following two questions:

Am I putting forth my utmost effort every day?

What actions can I take to improve my effort?

Determine your effort by beginning. Well, at the beginning. A poor beginning to the day will almost always hinder your success. In the 44 Super Bowl games, no team has ever returned from more than a 10-point deficit to triumph.

In the biggest event in sports history, no team has ever won despite a poor start. You can overcome your poor beginnings by identifying and resolving the issues that led to them in the first place.

To be dedicated to providing your finest effort, you must begin with the fundamentals. Get a decent night's sleep. If you feel sluggish and unproductive after only five hours of sleep per night, try getting six or seven hours. Leave home five minutes early to avoid the stress of rushing to be on time.

I once employed a woman in her early twenties. She was chronically tardy for work. That was unfortunate for her, given that my greatest pet peeve at work is tardiness.

When a person is chronically late to anything, particularly work, they communicate two things: their time is more important than mine and they are too lazy to get their act together and arrive at their destination on time. After many weeks of delay, I sat down with my employee to emphasize the importance of being on time.

I asked if she knew the time she needed to report to work. To her credit, she knew that her appointed arrival time was 8:30 a.m. it took her twenty minutes to travel from home to the office. On average, this girl was nearly twenty minutes late, which indicated that she did not leave her home until it was time for her to be at the office.

I merely advised her to leave her residence earlier. When she told me how much she had to do to get ready for work in the morning, I told her she needed to wake up earlier. If that was a concern, I advised her to consider retiring earlier the night before.

It is no longer my responsibility to enforce a restriction on my employees and I could see her irritation. I did not care when she went to sleep or woke up. I only cared that she arrived on time each morning. The delay was entirely under her control. She would have found a means to get to work on time if she had been dedicated.

Commit to learning something new every day. Make it a daily priority to observe or read something educational. Read a book or magazine to educate.

During leadership training, I ask participants to identify the three most recent books they have read. The participants must identify one skill, notion or concept from the book that can be applied to their jobs. Practical functions can be learned from almost any book read.

An employee once informed me that he lacked sufficient knowledge of mortgages. My training class was attended but still had concerns. He inquired more about government regulations and practices than our bank's policies and procedures. I instructed him to search for information online and peruse the Sunday newspaper's real estate section.

These were opportunities for him to take the initiative to learn something new, even outside of his regular work hours. I'm confident there are things you can do outside of work to dedicate yourself to improvement, depending on your field.

CHAPTER 12: HOW DOES ONE EVALUATE THEIR LEVEL OF SUCCESS WITH DEDICATION?

"How successful are you?" is one of the most often asked inquiries in the network marketing industry.

This question has always seemed perplexing to me. Before deciding to join, people want to know you've accomplished something with your business. However, even if you earn thousands of dollars daily, that doesn't necessarily imply they will either.

Personal dedication and accountability to your goals will determine whether you are successful in your business, not your sponsor's success.

Not only for the MLM industry but also for society, the fact that so many people equate success with wealth is a significant problem. Humans are materialistic by nature. If someone has a large home and a flashy car, it's clear that they're prosperous, right?

But what we might not know is that the individual may be discouraged. They may have all the nice toys and luxuries of wealth, but they may be forced to work eighty hours a week and have no leisure to enjoy them. Consequently, they don't perceive themselves to be successful.

On the other hand, a person may not have a sports car in the driveway, or a 4,000-square-foot home to sleep in but they are also not bound to a daily work schedule that compels them to exchange valuable time for meager wages. As a society, we would likely view this individual as unsuccessful or "against the grain." On a personal level, however, this individual may feel like the most successful individual in the universe.

Success is not solely based on monetary gain. Money is a side effect. People don't labor to get money because they desire it. They work to earn money to acquire the things that money can purchase. These items bring them joy and contentment is the primary key to achievement.

Perry Marshall states, "people who purchase a drill don't want one. "They desire a hole." To achieve success, you must set goals for yourself. For example, let me summarize the reasons for my success. Since I can remember, I have never liked laboring to make someone else wealthy. I was exchanging time for pay and all I had to show for it at the end of the week was a scribbled paycheck.

So, I set a goal of working for myself, building a business on my terms and ensuring that my efforts would contribute to MY prosperity, not someone else's.

I later reached a point where I was compelled to assess my situation. I am well-educated, experienced and possess leadership skills that can be used to coach, mentor and assist others in achieving their goals.

However, I was not utilizing these talents at my 9-to-5. I was becoming a slave to the system and overly reliant on a paycheck that, while it kept me solvent, made me miserable and could be taken away at any time.

I knew I had achieved my goal when I eventually decided to put my education to use and immerse myself in the network marketing industry full-time. I was aware of my accomplishment.

Why? Because I achieved my goal. I was no longer required to exchange my time for wages and report to a clueless supervisor. I was no longer required to endure a tedious commute to a location that made me wretched.

I was free to begin constructing my empire and doing just that.

Consider the many factors contributing to a person's success when deciding whether to join a network marketing opportunity with a specific individual. Remember that they may not be igniting the world. yet. Neither will you be, at least not initially.

You want to discover someone willing to collaborate with you and cares about your success. You seek a leader. someone who will assist you in achieving your goals for success.

How would you feel if you equated success with money, asked someone if they were successful and they replied, "OF COURSE! I'M MAKING TONS OF MONEY," only to find out later that they WEREN'T successful? This indicates that the individual did not care about you, as they lied to you. They were only concerned with their needs and would likely not be there when you needed them the most.

Any opportunity is only as valuable as its leaders. Not only do I have the opportunity to demonstrate my leadership abilities, but I am also surrounded by other leaders who share the same goals for success.

CHAPTER 13: A BETTER YOU: MY METHOD FOR LEARNING ANYTHING, ANYTIME, ANYWHERE.

So, you wish to improve yourself? What would you do if I told you that a method is available to you right now, as you read this, which enables you to know practically any life-improving subject piped directly into your brain - without lifting a finger or changing your daily regimen or way of life? Doesn't it sound like somebody has been viewing too much of "The Matrix"?

But as if that weren't enticing enough, imagine that before this information was transmitted into your mind, someone would devote their entire existence to learning everything possible about the topic.

They would cram years of experience, countless empirical studies, anecdotal observations, the science behind it and their knowledge of when to implement it directly into your head.

This technology is not science fiction; it exists. I have used it for three years, which has unquestionably enriched my life. It has inspired me to ascend mountains in distant lands, learn new exotic languages, improve my social skills and self-confidence, become more spiritually centered, acquire a more satisfying job, increase my finances and the list goes on.

Therefore, what is this miraculous technology that I'm describing that will make you a better person?

Audiobooks. You read that correctly; an MP3 device can play audiobooks (and I'm not talking about Harry Potter).

The description leading up to that anticlimactic revelation may have sounded sensationalist (which it was) but are we not now conditioned to respond to such language? The information age has, candidly, spoiled us.

We are now so spoiled that it is difficult to appreciate our incredible opportunities unless some smug marketers wrap it in a 'brand' and tell us it's great. To be interested in technology's possibilities, we must be persuaded that it is the latest fad or inundated by a Hollywood-style advertisement.

The practice of acquiring knowledge from literature is not novel. We have been doing it for countless millennia and it has served well, so why am I here extolling audiobooks as a revelation and the key to improving yourself? Based on my experience, their convenience makes them an unrivaled personal development instrument.

This modern era, in which we scarcely have time to rest, has made leisure time a more and more valuable commodity. This method of learning fits seamlessly into your existence. Your walk to work, the train commute, gathering up the kids and doing the dishes - you are squeezing more value out of these predetermined activities!

However, this extraordinary format's convenience doesn't end there. I carry a library of over twenty-five classic and contemporary self-improvement literature on my tiny 15GB MP3 player - the technology is amazing! This enables me to hold books on a vast array of topics with different potent and intriguing titles that provide you with the ultimate personal toolkit for bettering yourself:

I've discovered other, less apparent advantages to learning through spoken word. Hearing the author's words read aloud gives you a genuine sense of what they mean. You gain a better comprehension of the tone; certain words are highlighted, and the reader's enthusiasm can be both contagious and inspirational.

If you are interested in acquiring a new language, the benefits of hearing the pronunciation and inflections spoken aloud are self-evident. I should also mention this technology's more 'out there' applications for the more imaginative among us.

The popularity of hypnosis audio programs is on the rise, and there is also the comparatively new technology of 'binaural beats' designed to stimulate brainwaves. At the same time, I don't necessarily endorse it, it demonstrates the diversity of learning in this format.

So, what are the primary advantages of regularly listening to audiobooks for self-improvement?

How precisely will they help you become a better person?

Well, listening to one of the programs will not provide you with something as tangible as a master's degree or a pretentious qualification certificate but they can catalyze profound personal transformation.

I've discovered, for instance, that forming the habit of listening to a program during the 30-minute commute to work provides me with an empowering mindset for the remainder of that working day and that, over time, the newly acquired habits and beliefs will become fully internalized, allowing for different permanent behavioral changes. (Remember, this is without any alterations to my lifestyle, doesn't interfere with my free time and I have done nothing!)

Ultimately, suppose you want to be a better version of yourself. In that case, you must begin acting differently and I have provided you with the least effort-intensive instruments imaginable for achieving that goal. The most important point to convey is that excuses are no longer acceptable.

It is no longer acceptable to say, "I don't have the time" "I don't like reading" or "I can't afford it." Remind yourself that you haven't even attempted this yet and that this is as simple as it gets! If putting in earphones and simply listening seems too much effort, I suggest you require personal development audio more than anyone else.

CHAPTER 14: DO YOU DENY YOURSELF PERMISSION TO BE CREATIVE?

When not feeling at our most creative and free flowing, it's easy to turn to external factors to explain why our creativity is lacking.

However, you are the one person who can limit your creativity more than anyone else in the universe.

Most of the time, you are unaware of how and when you inhibit your creativity.

The issue boils down to permission.

Imagine a young boy being taken to a playground with a bewildering array of swings, slides, roundabouts, climbing frames and other thrilling apparatus to climb all over, in, out, around and through. Then, Jack is told that he can't use any apparatus because he is not permitted. He is permitted to observe the other children playing and having joy, but he is not permitted to join in.

Every day, Jack's parents bring him back to this playground and other equally thrilling and appealing playgrounds and each time Jack is told he can observe but not participate. Soon, Jack will lose all desire to visit the playground. He will only associate playground visits with frustration, disappointment, and misery.

The initial thing that comes to mind is likely Jack's plight. Your second thought may be, "What cruel parents, I would never treat my child that way!" But this is precisely what you do to your creativity when you deny it permission to explore and demonstrate its capabilities.

How then do you deny permission to your creativity and what can you do to change it?

The initial phase is to create consistently. When you devote a minimum amount of time to creating every day, you send a powerful message to your creativity: "Creativity is an integral part of my life." I devote daily time to my creative pursuits due to my importance to the creative process.

And naturally when you do this, your creativity comes to life, advances and has a blast. As Jack would if his parents said, "Go play Jack, you have an hour of free time and you can do whatever you want on the playground."

In addition to permitting yourself to be creative, it is essential to designate a space for creation. There is no need for a large artist's studio; many people work effectively with a basic desk and chair in the corner of a room.

It is important to devote this space specifically to your creativity. Like when you commit regular time, when you commit a specific space to your creative work, you communicate the importance of creating and giving your imagination permission to come out and play.

These two stages are essential for granting yourself creative permission.

Isn't it time you gave YOUR creativity - your inner Jack begging to come out and play - the permission it needs to demonstrate its capabilities?

CHAPTER 15: ARE YOU WILLING AND PREPARED TO IMPROVE WITH DEDICATION?

Instead of blaming and complaining about other people or situations, you would likely benefit in a very real manner from consistently focusing on IMPROVEMENT! To accomplish this, one must first be willing to conduct a thorough, goal, introspective examination of oneself from the neck up! Even though many claim to want to do so, few appear to be willing to commit to the necessary steps for achieving this goal.

After conducting personal development/self-help seminars for more than four decades, I firmly believe that unless/until one is willing to commit to all required, their potential for success is severely constrained! In light of this, this chapter will endeavor to consider, examine, review and discuss, using a mnemonic approach, what this signifies and represents and why it is significant.

1. Intelligence; concepts; imagine; innovate; integrity: Intelligence only matters if/when a person becomes wiser in a relevant, sustainable way by applying what he has heard, read and experienced wisely and intelligently!

He must recognize the distinction between his opinions and facts by committing to absolute integrity, especially when inconvenient! In this way, ideas make a difference because they enable meaningful innovation and the imagining of a diversity of options and alternatives!

2. Make an impression; motives; significance; goal: Specify your mission and explain why you feel strongly about particular issues! Proceed to make your impression on your self-improvement by understanding the significance of specific actions!

Why are certain things motivating you and why are your motivations advantageous and necessary?

3. Part of being introspective is having a strong sense of your mission and why it is important to you!

Personal priorities; planning; undertaking:

Do your priorities make you proud?

Will you participate in the essential procedure?

Everyone benefits when/if we learn and effectively employ high-quality, pertinent, sustainable planning!

4. Relevant, responsive, accountable; justifications: Avoid trivial matters and concentrate on important matters! How do you ensure that your responses are responsive to your concerns and requirements and that you are personally accountable for these? Utilize your finest reasoning to determine whether or not your motives are valid.

5. Options; opportunities; alternatives; an open mind: There are typically many options for the most advantageous method to proceed! Develop the ability

to recognize and evaluate multiple opportunities that may present themselves and if you don't feel strongly about any of them, create your own! Proceed and choose the optimal option for you!

6. Vision; views; value; values: How does your inner vision effectively address your actual, personal values? Why do you adhere to the opinions you hold?

7. Emphasis; endurance; energy/ energize; excellence: Instead of settling for mediocrity, strive for the highest level of personal excellence as often as feasible!

A sage once informed me that he was so successful because he outlived his contemporaries; therefore, he persevered rather than settling for the path of least resistance! When this focuses your attention, you will acquire personal energy and feel significantly more energized!

CHAPTER 16: BE DEDICATED TO YOUR CAUSE.

"At some point in everyone's existence, our inner fire goes out. It is then ignited by interaction with another human being. "We should all be grateful to those who rekindle our spirits," said Albert Schweitzer.

Dedication: the act of devoting or reserving for a specific purpose; devotion to a cause, ideal or goal. You are dedicated to your cause.

Those insurmountable obstacles lurk in the distance; they are the ones you can't seem to overcome. Friends, coworkers, colleagues, and family advise you to "forget about it." They tell you that you can't complete the task.

Unless you prevent them from doing so, they are destroying your aspirations. There are very few things that are genuinely impossible in life. Now I'm not talking about dunking a basketball when you're 5 feet and 5 inches tall.

I am referring to your aspirations. Things like starting a new business, completing a degree program (or beginning one), taking that trip you've always wanted to take, getting a new car or house, a promotion at work or getting a starting position (or perhaps a college scholarship) on a sports team.

Before the present, Norman Vincent Peale authored the book "Enthusiasm Makes The Difference." In the book, Peale outlined many practices that, if performed daily, would profoundly affect one's demeanor. These are the principles:

"Think a Good Day." What are your plans for the day? Do you spend a few minutes each morning reading, writing, and preparing for the upcoming day? You have a single opportunity to maximize the 24 hours you have been granted.

"Thank a Good Day." Native American prayer states, "Give thanks for unknown blessings already on their way." Many of us express gratitude for our benefits, but how many begin each day with gratitude and a positive outlook.

"Plan a Good Day." As a coach, I attempted to create the practice schedule for the week on Sunday. The following day, I could adjust the schedule as necessary. My daily and weekly master plans were in place. My daily master plan would consist of reviewing today's engagements and meetings, creating a task list and prioritizing the items based on their significance.

"Put Good into the Day" A good day consists of good thoughts, good actions and a positive attitude. Give five compliments daily, give without expecting anything in return, smile often, aid those who will never be able to repay you, buy someone lunch and assist a coworker or teammate with a problem.

Give your utmost effort. Remove from your vocabulary words such as can't, will not and what if?

Get up and get underway or, as our uncle used to say, Off and on. Get off your behind and onto your feet.

"Filled the Day with Enthusiasm" We teach our campers that Enthusiasm is "the God within you" at camp. Henry Ford had the following adage on his fireplace mantel:

"Anything is possible with enthusiasm." Enthusiasm is the yeast that propels hope into the heavens. Enthusiasm is the twinkle in your eye, the bounce in your step, the grasp on your hand, the irresistible will surge and the vigor with which you pursue your ideas. Enthusiasts are champions.

They are resolute. They possess durability. Enthusiasm is the foundation of all advancements! There is an accomplishment with it. Without it, only excuses exist."

The FAST Formula for Success is exactly what it sounds like, a method to help you reach your goals more quickly than you would without the FAST

Formula for Success. The acronym FAST stands for the following:

F: Determine why it is essential for you to achieve your goals and dreams. When your reason for doing something becomes sufficiently compelling, tenacity will follow but it must be YOUR goal or desire.

A: Act as if you are invincible, unconquerable and indisputable. Walk and speak with a Champion's Attitude

S: Visualize yourself accomplishing your goals in advance - Dream Big. If you are having difficulty visualizing what you are attempting to accomplish, find someone who already possesses the skill or attitude you wish to acquire. Spend time using this individual as a "mentor."

T: Take action toward achieving your goal. When a temporary roadblock throws you off course, you should retrace your steps, assess the situation and devise a method to circumvent the obstacle.

Great achievements just don't happen. Yes, occasionally, somebody makes it rich by winning the lottery. However, did you know that the most significant winners are broke and miserable within five years of winning the lottery?

Important accomplishments necessitate effort, training, practice, self-sacrifice, and discipline. To become the greatest athlete, one is capable of in athletics, one must devote countless hours to arduous, strenuous labor.

CONCLUSION.

Identifying, creating, and developing a balance between remaining true to oneself and achieving and pursuing what we perceive to be the best course of action is one of the most difficult challenges we face as individuals.

Do you consistently say what you mean, maintain absolute integrity, and feel good about what you've done, said, focused on and accomplished?

Are you ready to take a stand and be counted or are you a fence-straddler who avoids adopting a position until others do?

Are you influenced by polls, public opinion, and the desire to blend in or do you lead by example and motivate others to adopt your vision?

Do you know what you desire?

Do you possess a compelling, vital and vibrant vision that inspires you to pursue specific courses of action?

How much time, effort and energy have you invested in your self-awareness?

No one can ever be the greatest they can be until they define what that means for themselves, not for others. What makes you joyful and personally gratified and content?

Have you the courage to express your own opinion? Next time you are in a group, whether it be a business meeting, a tour group, acquaintances, etc., observe those who appear to spend most of their time trying to be as politically correct as possible!

Do you genuinely believe that you add something to a conversation or are you simply adopting the behavior of a literal sheep?

How can you feel good about yourself in the long-term if you spend time compromising your ideals and preferences?

What is more essential to you, the approval of others or your satisfaction with your actions?

Take some time to reflect: This is often one of the most difficult processes and procedures, as we often construct an artificial shell to make us more surface-happy (or satisfied). How much are you willing to be yourself? Do you have the fortitude to stand by your beliefs?

We often hear that we should strive to be the best we can be but how can we hope to achieve this if we don't prioritize being true to our convictions? What are you ready to do for yourself?

This book is part of an ongoing collection called "Laws of the Universe."

- Laws of Assumption.
- Law of Vibration
- Law of Polarity
- Law of Cause & Effect
- Law of Compensation
- Law of Correspondence
- Law of Divine Oneness
- Law of Rhythm
- Law of Perpetual Transmutation of Energy
- Law of Relativity
- Law of Inspiration
- Law of Gender and Gestation
- Law of Reciprocity
- Law of Purpose
- Law of Infinite Possibility
- Law of Unwavering Faith
- Law of Constant Motion
- Law of Analogy
- Law of Free Will
- Law of Expectation/Expectancy
- Law of Increase
- Law of Forgiveness
- Law of Sacrifice

- Law of Obedience
- Law of Non-Resistance
- Law of Action
- Law of Aspiration to a Higher Power
- Law of Charity
- Law of Compassion
- Law of Courage
- Law of Dedication
- Law of Faith
- Law of Generosity
- Law of Grace
- Law of Honesty
- Law of Hope
- Law of Job
- Law of Kindness
- Law of Leadership
- Law of Non-interference
- Law of Patience
- Law of Praise
- Law of Responsibility
- Law of Self Love
- Law of Thankfulness
- Law of Unconditional Love
- Parkinson's Law.

Other Series by Sherry Lee

"Spiritual Attraction."

- ➤ Ask, Believe, Receive.
- ➤ Faith Like a Mustard Seed.
- ➤ You Were Made for Such a Time as This.
- ➤ Let Go and Just Let God Handle it for You.
- ➤ You Have Not Because You Ask Not.
- ➤ Not my Will, Lord but Let Your Will be Done.
- ➤ Asking for This or Something Better.
- ➤ What is your Why.
- ➤ God said 365 Times in the Bible; DO NOT BE AFRAID.
- ➤ 10, 100, and 1,000 Fold Increase.
- ➤ Immeasurable More than I Can Hope or Imagine.
- ➤ All Things are Possible If you Believe.

"Opening and Balancing Your Chakra's"

- ➤ Unblocking your 3rd Eye
- ➤ Opening and Balancing your Heart Chakra
- ➤ Opening and Balancing your Crown Chakra
- ➤ Opening and Balancing your Throat Chakra
- ➤ Opening and Balancing your Solar Plexus Chakra

- ➢ Opening and Balancing your Sacral Chakra
- ➢ Opening and Balancing your Root Chakra.

"Why Alternative Medicine Works"

- ➢ Why Yoga Works
- ➢ Why Chakra Works
- ➢ Why Massage Therapy Works
- ➢ Why Reflexology Works
- ➢ Why Acupuncture Works
- ➢ Why Reiki Works
- ➢ Why Meditation Works
- ➢ Why Hypnosis Works
- ➢ Why Colon Cleansing Works
- ➢ Why NLP (Neuro Linguistic Programming) Works
- ➢ Why Energy Healing Works
- ➢ Why Foot Detoxing Works
- ➢ Why Singing Bowls Works.
- ➢ Why Tapping Works
- ➢ Why Muscle Testing Works.

"Using Sage and Smudging"

> Learning About Sage and Smudging
> Sage and Smudging for Love
> Sage and Smudging for Health and Healing
> Sage and Smudging for Wealth and Abundance
> Sage and Smudging for Spiritual Cleansing
> Sage and Smudging for Negativity.

"Learning About Crystals"

> Crystals for Love
> Crystals for Health
> Crystals for Wealth
> Crystals for Spiritual Cleansing
> Crystals for Removing Negativity.

"What Every Newlywed Should Know and Discuss Before Marriage."

> Newlywed Communication on Money
> Newlywed Communication on In-laws
> Newlywed Communication about Children.
> Newlywed Communication on Religion.
> Newlywed Communication on Friends.

- ➢ Newlywed Communication on Retirement.
- ➢ Newlywed Communication on Sex.
- ➢ Newlywed Communication on Boundaries.
- ➢ Newlywed Communication on Roles and Responsibilities.

"Health is Wealth."

- ➢ Health is Wealth
- ➢ Positivity is Wealth
- ➢ Emotions are Wealth.
- ➢ Social Health is Wealth.
- ➢ Happiness is Wealth.
- ➢ Fitness is Wealth.
- ➢ Meditating is Wealth.
- ➢ Communication is Wealth.
- ➢ Mental Health is Wealth.
- ➢ Gratitude is Wealth.

"Personal Development Collection."

- ➢ Manifesting for Beginners
- ➢ Crystals for Beginners
- ➢ How to Manifest More Money into Your Life.
- ➢ How to work from home more effectively.
- ➢ How to Accomplish More in Less Time.
- ➢ How to End Procrastination.

- Learning to Praise and acknowledge your Accomplishments.
- How to Become Your Own Driving Force.
- Creating a Confident Persona.
- How to Meditate.
- How to Set Affirmations.
- How to Set and Achieve Your Goals.
- Achieving Your Fitness Goals.
- Achieving Your Weight Loss Goals.
- How to Create an Effective Vision Board.

Other Books By Sherry Lee:

- Repeating Angel Numbers
- Most Popular Archangels.
- ASKFFIRMATION & AFFORMATION: The Art of Asking and Receiving What You Want and Desire
- COLLAPSING TIME FOR SUPERNATURAL MANIFESTATION.
- One Word for a Year or Just a Quarter: Helping your Life and Business to be More Effective.
- 369 Manifestation Method
- 66 Ways to be More Productive in the Morning

- ➢ 66 Ways to be More Productive in the Evening.
- ➢ Women Can be Wealthy at Any Age.

Author Bio

Sherry Lee. Sherry enjoys reading personal development books, so she decided to write about something she is passionate about. More books will come in this collection, so follow her on Amazon for more books.

Thank you for your purchase of this book.

I appreciate you, my excellent customer.

God Bless You.

Sherry Lee.

Made in the USA
Columbia, SC
07 January 2024

30014340R00075